# 50 Sweet and Savory Jam Recipes for Home

By: Kelly Johnson

# Table of Contents

- Classic Strawberry Jam
- Blueberry Lemon Jam
- Raspberry Peach Jam
- Apricot Vanilla Jam
- Spiced Apple Butter
- Cherry Almond Jam
- Mango Ginger Jam
- Pineapple Jalapeno Jam
- Cranberry Orange Jam
- Fig Balsamic Jam
- Plum Cardamom Jam
- Blackberry Sage Jam
- Kiwi Lime Jam
- Strawberry Rhubarb Jam
- Pear Ginger Jam
- Peach Bourbon Jam
- Mixed Berry Chia Jam
- Orange Marmalade
- Tomato Basil Jam
- Jalapeno Peach Jam
- Raspberry Chipotle Jam
- Blueberry Lavender Jam
- Strawberry Basil Jam
- Cranberry Jalapeno Jam
- Ginger Pear Jam
- Pineapple Coconut Jam
- Apricot Rosemary Jam
- Mango Habanero Jam
- Peach Thyme Jam
- Blackberry Lemon Thyme Jam
- Raspberry Vanilla Bean Jam
- Cherry Lime Jam
- Grapefruit Rose Jam
- Pear Cardamom Jam
- Strawberry Mint Jam

- Blueberry Lime Jam
- Pineapple Mango Jam
- Peach Jalapeno Jam
- Tomato Peach Jam
- Raspberry Jalapeno Jam
- Strawberry Rhubarb Ginger Jam
- Apple Cinnamon Jam
- Plum Port Jam
- Blueberry Lemon Verbena Jam
- Peach Basil Jam
- Cherry Bourbon Jam
- Strawberry Coconut Jam
- Mango Lime Chili Jam
- Pineapple Sage Jam
- Orange Ginger Jam

**Classic Strawberry Jam**

Ingredients:

- 2 pounds (about 900g) fresh strawberries, hulled and chopped
- 2 cups (400g) granulated sugar
- 2 tablespoons (30ml) fresh lemon juice

Instructions:

1. In a large, heavy-bottomed pot, combine the chopped strawberries, sugar, and lemon juice.
2. Stir the mixture well to combine, then let it sit for about 10-15 minutes to allow the strawberries to release their juices.
3. Place the pot over medium-high heat and bring the mixture to a boil, stirring frequently.
4. Once the mixture reaches a boil, reduce the heat to medium-low and let it simmer, stirring occasionally, until it thickens and reaches the desired consistency. This typically takes about 20-30 minutes.
5. To test if the jam is ready, place a small amount on a chilled plate and let it cool for a minute. If it wrinkles when you push it with your finger, it's ready.
6. Once the jam reaches the desired consistency, remove it from the heat and let it cool slightly.
7. Transfer the jam to clean, sterilized jars, leaving a little space at the top. Seal the jars tightly.
8. Let the jars cool completely at room temperature, then store them in the refrigerator for up to several weeks. If you'd like to store them for longer, you can process the jars in a water bath for proper canning.

This Classic Strawberry Jam is perfect for spreading on toast, scones, or biscuits, or for using in various dessert recipes. Enjoy!

**Blueberry Lemon Jam**

Ingredients:

- 4 cups (about 600g) fresh blueberries
- 2 cups (400g) granulated sugar
- Zest and juice of 1 lemon
- 1 tablespoon (15ml) lemon juice (optional, for extra tang)

Instructions:

1. Rinse the blueberries and remove any stems.
2. In a large, heavy-bottomed pot, combine the blueberries, sugar, lemon zest, and lemon juice (if using).
3. Stir the mixture well to combine, then let it sit for about 10-15 minutes to allow the blueberries to release their juices.
4. Place the pot over medium-high heat and bring the mixture to a boil, stirring frequently.
5. Once the mixture reaches a boil, reduce the heat to medium-low and let it simmer, stirring occasionally, until it thickens and reaches the desired consistency. This typically takes about 20-30 minutes.
6. To test if the jam is ready, place a small amount on a chilled plate and let it cool for a minute. If it wrinkles when you push it with your finger, it's ready.
7. Once the jam reaches the desired consistency, remove it from the heat and let it cool slightly.
8. Transfer the jam to clean, sterilized jars, leaving a little space at the top. Seal the jars tightly.
9. Let the jars cool completely at room temperature, then store them in the refrigerator for up to several weeks. If you'd like to store them for longer, you can process the jars in a water bath for proper canning.

This Blueberry Lemon Jam is perfect for spreading on toast, pancakes, or yogurt, or for using as a filling in pastries or cakes. Enjoy the sweet and tangy flavors!

**Raspberry Peach Jam**

Ingredients:

- 4 cups (about 600g) fresh raspberries
- 4 cups (about 600g) peeled and chopped ripe peaches
- 4 cups (800g) granulated sugar
- Juice of 1 lemon
- 1 package (1.75 oz/49g) powdered fruit pectin

Instructions:

1. Prepare your canning jars and lids according to proper canning procedures.
2. In a large, heavy-bottomed pot, combine the raspberries, peaches, and lemon juice.
3. Use a potato masher or fork to gently mash the fruit, leaving some chunks for texture.
4. Stir in the powdered fruit pectin until well combined.
5. Place the pot over medium-high heat and bring the mixture to a full rolling boil, stirring constantly.
6. Add the sugar all at once, stirring until dissolved.
7. Return the mixture to a full rolling boil, stirring constantly. Boil for exactly 1 minute, then remove the pot from the heat.
8. Skim off any foam from the surface of the jam using a spoon.
9. Ladle the hot jam into prepared jars, leaving about 1/4 inch of headspace.
10. Wipe the rims of the jars with a clean, damp cloth to remove any residue.
11. Place the lids on the jars and screw on the bands until fingertip tight.
12. Process the filled jars in a boiling water canner for 10 minutes (adjust for altitude if necessary).
13. Remove the jars from the canner and let them cool completely at room temperature. Check the seals before storing.
14. Store the jars in a cool, dark place for up to a year. Once opened, store in the refrigerator and use within a few weeks.

This Raspberry Peach Jam is perfect for spreading on toast, muffins, or scones, or for using as a topping for yogurt or ice cream. Enjoy the delicious combination of sweet raspberries and juicy peaches!

**Apricot Vanilla Jam**

Ingredients:

- 2 pounds (about 900g) ripe apricots, pitted and chopped
- 2 cups (400g) granulated sugar
- Juice of 1 lemon
- 1 vanilla bean, split lengthwise and seeds scraped (or 1 teaspoon vanilla extract)

Instructions:

1. Prepare your canning jars and lids according to proper canning procedures.
2. In a large, heavy-bottomed pot, combine the chopped apricots, sugar, lemon juice, and vanilla bean seeds (or vanilla extract).
3. Stir the mixture well to combine.
4. Place the pot over medium-high heat and bring the mixture to a full rolling boil, stirring constantly.
5. Reduce the heat to medium-low and let the mixture simmer, stirring occasionally, until it thickens and reaches the desired consistency. This typically takes about 20-30 minutes.
6. To test if the jam is ready, place a small amount on a chilled plate and let it cool for a minute. If it wrinkles when you push it with your finger, it's ready.
7. Once the jam reaches the desired consistency, remove the pot from the heat.
8. Remove the vanilla bean from the jam, if using.
9. Ladle the hot jam into prepared jars, leaving about 1/4 inch of headspace.
10. Wipe the rims of the jars with a clean, damp cloth to remove any residue.
11. Place the lids on the jars and screw on the bands until fingertip tight.
12. Process the filled jars in a boiling water canner for 10 minutes (adjust for altitude if necessary).
13. Remove the jars from the canner and let them cool completely at room temperature. Check the seals before storing.
14. Store the jars in a cool, dark place for up to a year. Once opened, store in the refrigerator and use within a few weeks.

This Apricot Vanilla Jam is perfect for spreading on toast, biscuits, or croissants, or for using as a filling in pastries or cakes. Enjoy the delightful combination of sweet apricots and fragrant vanilla!

**Spiced Apple Butter**

Ingredients:

- 5 pounds (about 2.25 kg) apples, peeled, cored, and chopped (use a mix of sweet and tart varieties)
- 2 cups (400g) granulated sugar
- 1 cup (200g) packed brown sugar
- 2 teaspoons ground cinnamon
- 1/2 teaspoon ground nutmeg
- 1/4 teaspoon ground cloves
- 1/4 teaspoon ground allspice
- Juice of 1 lemon
- Pinch of salt

Instructions:

1. Place the chopped apples in a slow cooker.
2. In a separate bowl, combine the granulated sugar, brown sugar, cinnamon, nutmeg, cloves, allspice, lemon juice, and salt. Stir until well combined.
3. Pour the sugar and spice mixture over the apples in the slow cooker and stir to coat the apples evenly.
4. Cover the slow cooker and cook the apples on low heat for about 10-12 hours, stirring occasionally, until the mixture is thick and darkened in color.
5. Once the apple mixture has cooked down and thickened, remove the lid from the slow cooker and continue cooking for an additional 1-2 hours on low heat, stirring occasionally, to further thicken the apple butter.
6. Once the apple butter has reached the desired consistency, remove it from the heat and let it cool slightly.
7. Use an immersion blender or transfer the mixture to a blender or food processor and blend until smooth.
8. If you prefer a smoother texture, you can strain the apple butter through a fine mesh sieve to remove any remaining chunks.
9. Transfer the apple butter to clean, sterilized jars, leaving about 1/4 inch of headspace.
10. Wipe the rims of the jars with a clean, damp cloth to remove any residue.
11. Place the lids on the jars and screw on the bands until fingertip tight.

12. Process the filled jars in a boiling water canner for 10 minutes (adjust for altitude if necessary).
13. Remove the jars from the canner and let them cool completely at room temperature. Check the seals before storing.
14. Store the jars in a cool, dark place for up to a year. Once opened, store in the refrigerator and use within a few weeks.

This Spiced Apple Butter is perfect for spreading on toast, muffins, or biscuits, or for using as a topping for pancakes or oatmeal. Enjoy the warm and cozy flavors of fall!

**Cherry Almond Jam**

Ingredients:

- 4 cups (about 600g) fresh cherries, pitted and chopped
- 2 cups (400g) granulated sugar
- Juice of 1 lemon
- 1 teaspoon almond extract
- 1 package (1.75 oz/49g) powdered fruit pectin

Instructions:

1. Prepare your canning jars and lids according to proper canning procedures.
2. In a large, heavy-bottomed pot, combine the chopped cherries, sugar, lemon juice, and almond extract.
3. Stir the mixture well to combine.
4. Place the pot over medium-high heat and bring the mixture to a full rolling boil, stirring constantly.
5. Add the powdered fruit pectin, stirring until dissolved.
6. Return the mixture to a full rolling boil, stirring constantly. Boil for exactly 1 minute, then remove the pot from the heat.
7. Skim off any foam from the surface of the jam using a spoon.
8. Ladle the hot jam into prepared jars, leaving about 1/4 inch of headspace.
9. Wipe the rims of the jars with a clean, damp cloth to remove any residue.
10. Place the lids on the jars and screw on the bands until fingertip tight.
11. Process the filled jars in a boiling water canner for 10 minutes (adjust for altitude if necessary).
12. Remove the jars from the canner and let them cool completely at room temperature. Check the seals before storing.
13. Store the jars in a cool, dark place for up to a year. Once opened, store in the refrigerator and use within a few weeks.

This Cherry Almond Jam is perfect for spreading on toast, scones, or pancakes, or for using as a filling in pastries or thumbprint cookies. Enjoy the sweet and nutty flavors!

**Mango Ginger Jam**

Ingredients:

- 4 cups (about 600g) ripe mangoes, peeled, pitted, and chopped
- 2 cups (400g) granulated sugar
- Juice and zest of 1 lemon
- 2 tablespoons freshly grated ginger
- 1 package (1.75 oz/49g) powdered fruit pectin

Instructions:

1. Prepare your canning jars and lids according to proper canning procedures.
2. In a large, heavy-bottomed pot, combine the chopped mangoes, sugar, lemon juice, lemon zest, and grated ginger.
3. Stir the mixture well to combine.
4. Place the pot over medium-high heat and bring the mixture to a full rolling boil, stirring constantly.
5. Add the powdered fruit pectin, stirring until dissolved.
6. Return the mixture to a full rolling boil, stirring constantly. Boil for exactly 1 minute, then remove the pot from the heat.
7. Skim off any foam from the surface of the jam using a spoon.
8. Ladle the hot jam into prepared jars, leaving about 1/4 inch of headspace.
9. Wipe the rims of the jars with a clean, damp cloth to remove any residue.
10. Place the lids on the jars and screw on the bands until fingertip tight.
11. Process the filled jars in a boiling water canner for 10 minutes (adjust for altitude if necessary).
12. Remove the jars from the canner and let them cool completely at room temperature. Check the seals before storing.
13. Store the jars in a cool, dark place for up to a year. Once opened, store in the refrigerator and use within a few weeks.

This Mango Ginger Jam is perfect for spreading on toast, muffins, or yogurt, or for using as a topping for ice cream or cheesecake. Enjoy the tropical and spicy flavors!

**Pineapple Jalapeno Jam**

Ingredients:

- 4 cups (about 600g) fresh pineapple, diced
- 2 cups (400g) granulated sugar
- Juice and zest of 2 limes
- 2 jalapeno peppers, seeded and finely chopped
- 1 package (1.75 oz/49g) powdered fruit pectin

Instructions:

1. Prepare your canning jars and lids according to proper canning procedures.
2. In a large, heavy-bottomed pot, combine the diced pineapple, sugar, lime juice, lime zest, and chopped jalapeno peppers.
3. Stir the mixture well to combine.
4. Place the pot over medium-high heat and bring the mixture to a full rolling boil, stirring constantly.
5. Add the powdered fruit pectin, stirring until dissolved.
6. Return the mixture to a full rolling boil, stirring constantly. Boil for exactly 1 minute, then remove the pot from the heat.
7. Skim off any foam from the surface of the jam using a spoon.
8. Ladle the hot jam into prepared jars, leaving about 1/4 inch of headspace.
9. Wipe the rims of the jars with a clean, damp cloth to remove any residue.
10. Place the lids on the jars and screw on the bands until fingertip tight.
11. Process the filled jars in a boiling water canner for 10 minutes (adjust for altitude if necessary).
12. Remove the jars from the canner and let them cool completely at room temperature. Check the seals before storing.
13. Store the jars in a cool, dark place for up to a year. Once opened, store in the refrigerator and use within a few weeks.

This Pineapple Jalapeno Jam is perfect for spreading on crackers, sandwiches, or grilled meats, or for using as a glaze for chicken or fish. Enjoy the sweet and spicy flavors!

**Cranberry Orange Jam**

Ingredients:

- 4 cups (about 450g) fresh or frozen cranberries
- 2 cups (400g) granulated sugar
- Zest and juice of 2 oranges
- 1/2 cup (120ml) water
- 1 package (1.75 oz/49g) powdered fruit pectin

Instructions:

1. Prepare your canning jars and lids according to proper canning procedures.
2. In a large, heavy-bottomed pot, combine the cranberries, sugar, orange zest, orange juice, and water.
3. Stir the mixture well to combine.
4. Place the pot over medium-high heat and bring the mixture to a full rolling boil, stirring constantly.
5. Add the powdered fruit pectin, stirring until dissolved.
6. Return the mixture to a full rolling boil, stirring constantly. Boil for exactly 1 minute, then remove the pot from the heat.
7. Skim off any foam from the surface of the jam using a spoon.
8. Ladle the hot jam into prepared jars, leaving about 1/4 inch of headspace.
9. Wipe the rims of the jars with a clean, damp cloth to remove any residue.
10. Place the lids on the jars and screw on the bands until fingertip tight.
11. Process the filled jars in a boiling water canner for 10 minutes (adjust for altitude if necessary).
12. Remove the jars from the canner and let them cool completely at room temperature. Check the seals before storing.
13. Store the jars in a cool, dark place for up to a year. Once opened, store in the refrigerator and use within a few weeks.

This Cranberry Orange Jam is perfect for spreading on toast, muffins, or scones, or for using as a filling in pastries or thumbprint cookies. Enjoy the tangy and citrusy flavors!

**Fig Balsamic Jam**

Ingredients:

- 2 pounds (about 900g) fresh figs, stemmed and chopped
- 1 1/2 cups (300g) granulated sugar
- 1/4 cup (60ml) balsamic vinegar
- Juice of 1 lemon
- 1/2 teaspoon vanilla extract (optional)

Instructions:

1. Prepare your canning jars and lids according to proper canning procedures.
2. In a large, heavy-bottomed pot, combine the chopped figs, sugar, balsamic vinegar, and lemon juice.
3. Stir the mixture well to combine.
4. Place the pot over medium-high heat and bring the mixture to a full rolling boil, stirring constantly.
5. Once the mixture reaches a boil, reduce the heat to medium-low and let it simmer, stirring occasionally, until it thickens and reaches the desired consistency. This typically takes about 30-40 minutes.
6. To test if the jam is ready, place a small amount on a chilled plate and let it cool for a minute. If it wrinkles when you push it with your finger, it's ready.
7. Once the jam reaches the desired consistency, remove the pot from the heat.
8. Stir in the vanilla extract, if using.
9. Ladle the hot jam into prepared jars, leaving about 1/4 inch of headspace.
10. Wipe the rims of the jars with a clean, damp cloth to remove any residue.
11. Place the lids on the jars and screw on the bands until fingertip tight.
12. Process the filled jars in a boiling water canner for 10 minutes (adjust for altitude if necessary).
13. Remove the jars from the canner and let them cool completely at room temperature. Check the seals before storing.
14. Store the jars in a cool, dark place for up to a year. Once opened, store in the refrigerator and use within a few weeks.

This Fig Balsamic Jam is perfect for spreading on bread, crackers, or cheese, or for using as a glaze for meats or vegetables. Enjoy the sweet and tangy flavors!

**Plum Cardamom Jam**

Ingredients:

- 4 cups (about 900g) ripe plums, pitted and chopped
- 2 cups (400g) granulated sugar
- Juice and zest of 1 lemon
- 1 teaspoon ground cardamom
- 1/2 teaspoon vanilla extract (optional)

Instructions:

1. Prepare your canning jars and lids according to proper canning procedures.
2. In a large, heavy-bottomed pot, combine the chopped plums, sugar, lemon juice, lemon zest, and ground cardamom.
3. Stir the mixture well to combine.
4. Place the pot over medium-high heat and bring the mixture to a full rolling boil, stirring constantly.
5. Once the mixture reaches a boil, reduce the heat to medium-low and let it simmer, stirring occasionally, until it thickens and reaches the desired consistency. This typically takes about 30-40 minutes.
6. To test if the jam is ready, place a small amount on a chilled plate and let it cool for a minute. If it wrinkles when you push it with your finger, it's ready.
7. Once the jam reaches the desired consistency, remove the pot from the heat.
8. Stir in the vanilla extract, if using.
9. Ladle the hot jam into prepared jars, leaving about 1/4 inch of headspace.
10. Wipe the rims of the jars with a clean, damp cloth to remove any residue.
11. Place the lids on the jars and screw on the bands until fingertip tight.
12. Process the filled jars in a boiling water canner for 10 minutes (adjust for altitude if necessary).
13. Remove the jars from the canner and let them cool completely at room temperature. Check the seals before storing.
14. Store the jars in a cool, dark place for up to a year. Once opened, store in the refrigerator and use within a few weeks.

This Plum Cardamom Jam is perfect for spreading on toast, muffins, or scones, or for using as a filling in pastries or cakes. Enjoy the sweet and aromatic flavors!

**Blackberry Sage Jam**

Ingredients:

- 4 cups (about 600g) fresh blackberries
- 2 cups (400g) granulated sugar
- Juice and zest of 1 lemon
- 2 tablespoons finely chopped fresh sage leaves

Instructions:

1. Prepare your canning jars and lids according to proper canning procedures.
2. In a large, heavy-bottomed pot, combine the blackberries, sugar, lemon juice, lemon zest, and chopped sage leaves.
3. Stir the mixture well to combine.
4. Place the pot over medium-high heat and bring the mixture to a full rolling boil, stirring constantly.
5. Once the mixture reaches a boil, reduce the heat to medium-low and let it simmer, stirring occasionally, until it thickens and reaches the desired consistency. This typically takes about 20-30 minutes.
6. To test if the jam is ready, place a small amount on a chilled plate and let it cool for a minute. If it wrinkles when you push it with your finger, it's ready.
7. Once the jam reaches the desired consistency, remove the pot from the heat.
8. Ladle the hot jam into prepared jars, leaving about 1/4 inch of headspace.
9. Wipe the rims of the jars with a clean, damp cloth to remove any residue.
10. Place the lids on the jars and screw on the bands until fingertip tight.
11. Process the filled jars in a boiling water canner for 10 minutes (adjust for altitude if necessary).
12. Remove the jars from the canner and let them cool completely at room temperature. Check the seals before storing.
13. Store the jars in a cool, dark place for up to a year. Once opened, store in the refrigerator and use within a few weeks.

This Blackberry Sage Jam is perfect for spreading on toast, biscuits, or cheese, or for using as a glaze for meats. Enjoy the sweet and savory flavors!

**Kiwi Lime Jam**

Ingredients:

- 2 pounds (about 900g) ripe kiwifruit, peeled and diced
- 1 cup (200g) granulated sugar
- Juice and zest of 2 limes

Instructions:

1. Prepare your canning jars and lids according to proper canning procedures.
2. In a large, heavy-bottomed pot, combine the diced kiwifruit, sugar, lime juice, and lime zest.
3. Stir the mixture well to combine.
4. Place the pot over medium-high heat and bring the mixture to a full rolling boil, stirring constantly.
5. Reduce the heat to medium-low and let the mixture simmer, stirring occasionally, until it thickens and reaches the desired consistency. This typically takes about 20-30 minutes.
6. To test if the jam is ready, place a small amount on a chilled plate and let it cool for a minute. If it wrinkles when you push it with your finger, it's ready.
7. Once the jam reaches the desired consistency, remove the pot from the heat.
8. Ladle the hot jam into prepared jars, leaving about 1/4 inch of headspace.
9. Wipe the rims of the jars with a clean, damp cloth to remove any residue.
10. Place the lids on the jars and screw on the bands until fingertip tight.
11. Process the filled jars in a boiling water canner for 10 minutes (adjust for altitude if necessary).
12. Remove the jars from the canner and let them cool completely at room temperature. Check the seals before storing.
13. Store the jars in a cool, dark place for up to a year. Once opened, store in the refrigerator and use within a few weeks.

This Kiwi Lime Jam is perfect for spreading on toast, muffins, or scones, or for using as a topping for yogurt or ice cream. Enjoy the refreshing flavors!

**Strawberry Rhubarb Jam**

Ingredients:

- 4 cups (about 450g) fresh rhubarb, diced
- 4 cups (about 600g) fresh strawberries, hulled and sliced
- 4 cups (800g) granulated sugar
- Juice and zest of 1 lemon

Instructions:

1. Prepare your canning jars and lids according to proper canning procedures.
2. In a large, heavy-bottomed pot, combine the diced rhubarb, sliced strawberries, sugar, lemon juice, and lemon zest.
3. Stir the mixture well to combine.
4. Place the pot over medium-high heat and bring the mixture to a full rolling boil, stirring constantly.
5. Once the mixture reaches a boil, reduce the heat to medium-low and let it simmer, stirring occasionally, until it thickens and reaches the desired consistency. This typically takes about 20-30 minutes.
6. To test if the jam is ready, place a small amount on a chilled plate and let it cool for a minute. If it wrinkles when you push it with your finger, it's ready.
7. Once the jam reaches the desired consistency, remove the pot from the heat.
8. Ladle the hot jam into prepared jars, leaving about 1/4 inch of headspace.
9. Wipe the rims of the jars with a clean, damp cloth to remove any residue.
10. Place the lids on the jars and screw on the bands until fingertip tight.
11. Process the filled jars in a boiling water canner for 10 minutes (adjust for altitude if necessary).
12. Remove the jars from the canner and let them cool completely at room temperature. Check the seals before storing.
13. Store the jars in a cool, dark place for up to a year. Once opened, store in the refrigerator and use within a few weeks.

This Strawberry Rhubarb Jam is perfect for spreading on toast, muffins, or scones, or for using as a filling in pies or tarts. Enjoy the sweet and tart flavors!

**Pear Ginger Jam**

Ingredients:

- 4 cups (about 900g) ripe pears, peeled, cored, and chopped
- 2 cups (400g) granulated sugar
- Juice and zest of 1 lemon
- 2 tablespoons finely chopped fresh ginger

Instructions:

1. Prepare your canning jars and lids according to proper canning procedures.
2. In a large, heavy-bottomed pot, combine the chopped pears, sugar, lemon juice, lemon zest, and chopped ginger.
3. Stir the mixture well to combine.
4. Place the pot over medium-high heat and bring the mixture to a full rolling boil, stirring constantly.
5. Once the mixture reaches a boil, reduce the heat to medium-low and let it simmer, stirring occasionally, until it thickens and reaches the desired consistency. This typically takes about 20-30 minutes.
6. To test if the jam is ready, place a small amount on a chilled plate and let it cool for a minute. If it wrinkles when you push it with your finger, it's ready.
7. Once the jam reaches the desired consistency, remove the pot from the heat.
8. Ladle the hot jam into prepared jars, leaving about 1/4 inch of headspace.
9. Wipe the rims of the jars with a clean, damp cloth to remove any residue.
10. Place the lids on the jars and screw on the bands until fingertip tight.
11. Process the filled jars in a boiling water canner for 10 minutes (adjust for altitude if necessary).
12. Remove the jars from the canner and let them cool completely at room temperature. Check the seals before storing.
13. Store the jars in a cool, dark place for up to a year. Once opened, store in the refrigerator and use within a few weeks.

This Pear Ginger Jam is perfect for spreading on toast, muffins, or scones, or for using as a filling in pastries or thumbprint cookies. Enjoy the sweet and spicy flavors!

**Peach Bourbon Jam**

Ingredients:

- 4 cups (about 900g) ripe peaches, peeled, pitted, and chopped
- 2 cups (400g) granulated sugar
- 1/4 cup (60ml) bourbon
- Juice and zest of 1 lemon

Instructions:

1. Prepare your canning jars and lids according to proper canning procedures.
2. In a large, heavy-bottomed pot, combine the chopped peaches, sugar, bourbon, lemon juice, and lemon zest.
3. Stir the mixture well to combine.
4. Place the pot over medium-high heat and bring the mixture to a full rolling boil, stirring constantly.
5. Once the mixture reaches a boil, reduce the heat to medium-low and let it simmer, stirring occasionally, until it thickens and reaches the desired consistency. This typically takes about 20-30 minutes.
6. To test if the jam is ready, place a small amount on a chilled plate and let it cool for a minute. If it wrinkles when you push it with your finger, it's ready.
7. Once the jam reaches the desired consistency, remove the pot from the heat.
8. Ladle the hot jam into prepared jars, leaving about 1/4 inch of headspace.
9. Wipe the rims of the jars with a clean, damp cloth to remove any residue.
10. Place the lids on the jars and screw on the bands until fingertip tight.
11. Process the filled jars in a boiling water canner for 10 minutes (adjust for altitude if necessary).
12. Remove the jars from the canner and let them cool completely at room temperature. Check the seals before storing.
13. Store the jars in a cool, dark place for up to a year. Once opened, store in the refrigerator and use within a few weeks.

This Peach Bourbon Jam is perfect for spreading on toast, biscuits, or pancakes, or for using as a glaze for grilled meats. Enjoy the sweet and boozy flavors!

**Mixed Berry Chia Jam**

Ingredients:

- 3 cups mixed berries (such as strawberries, blueberries, raspberries, blackberries), fresh or frozen
- 3-4 tablespoons maple syrup or honey, adjust to taste
- 2 tablespoons chia seeds
- Juice of 1 lemon

Instructions:

1. In a medium saucepan, combine the mixed berries and lemon juice over medium heat. If using frozen berries, let them thaw slightly.
2. Cook the berries, stirring occasionally, until they start to break down and release their juices, about 5-7 minutes.
3. Mash the berries with a fork or potato masher to your desired consistency.
4. Stir in the maple syrup or honey, adjusting the sweetness to your taste.
5. Add the chia seeds and continue to cook the mixture for another 5 minutes, stirring frequently, until the jam thickens.
6. Remove the saucepan from the heat and let the jam cool for a few minutes.
7. Transfer the jam to clean, sterilized jars.
8. Let the jam cool completely before sealing the jars.
9. Store the jam in the refrigerator for up to 2 weeks.

This Mixed Berry Chia Jam is perfect for spreading on toast, pancakes, yogurt, or oatmeal. Enjoy the delicious and nutritious flavors!

**Orange Marmalade**

Ingredients:

- 4 large oranges
- 1 lemon
- 8 cups (1600g) granulated sugar
- 8 cups water

Instructions:

1. Wash the oranges and lemon thoroughly. Cut the oranges and lemon in half, then into thin slices, removing any seeds as you go. If you prefer a smoother marmalade, you can remove the pulp from half of the orange slices.
2. In a large pot, combine the sliced oranges and lemon with the water. Bring to a boil over medium-high heat, then reduce the heat and simmer for about 40-45 minutes, or until the fruit is soft and the peel is tender.
3. Once the fruit is tender, add the sugar to the pot, stirring until dissolved.
4. Increase the heat to medium-high and bring the mixture to a rapid boil. Cook, stirring frequently, until the marmalade thickens and reaches the desired consistency. This usually takes about 15-20 minutes.
5. To test if the marmalade is ready, place a small amount on a chilled plate and let it cool for a minute. If it wrinkles when you push it with your finger, it's ready.
6. Once the marmalade is ready, remove the pot from the heat.
7. Ladle the hot marmalade into clean, sterilized jars, leaving about 1/4 inch of headspace.
8. Wipe the rims of the jars with a clean, damp cloth to remove any residue.
9. Place the lids on the jars and screw on the bands until fingertip tight.
10. Process the filled jars in a boiling water canner for 10 minutes (adjust for altitude if necessary).
11. Remove the jars from the canner and let them cool completely at room temperature. Check the seals before storing.
12. Store the jars in a cool, dark place for up to a year. Once opened, store in the refrigerator and use within a few weeks.

This Orange Marmalade is perfect for spreading on toast, scones, or muffins. Enjoy the bright and citrusy flavor!

**Tomato Basil Jam**

Ingredients:

- 2 pounds (about 900g) ripe tomatoes, peeled, seeded, and chopped
- 1 cup (200g) granulated sugar
- Juice of 1 lemon
- Zest of 1 lemon
- 2 tablespoons balsamic vinegar
- 1/4 cup (10g) fresh basil leaves, chopped
- Pinch of salt

Instructions:

1. Prepare your canning jars and lids according to proper canning procedures.
2. In a large, heavy-bottomed pot, combine the chopped tomatoes, sugar, lemon juice, lemon zest, and balsamic vinegar.
3. Stir the mixture well to combine.
4. Place the pot over medium-high heat and bring the mixture to a full rolling boil, stirring constantly.
5. Reduce the heat to medium-low and let the mixture simmer, stirring occasionally, until it thickens and reaches the desired consistency. This typically takes about 40-50 minutes.
6. Stir in the chopped basil leaves and a pinch of salt, and continue to cook for an additional 5 minutes.
7. To test if the jam is ready, place a small amount on a chilled plate and let it cool for a minute. If it wrinkles when you push it with your finger, it's ready.
8. Once the jam reaches the desired consistency, remove the pot from the heat.
9. Ladle the hot jam into prepared jars, leaving about 1/4 inch of headspace.
10. Wipe the rims of the jars with a clean, damp cloth to remove any residue.
11. Place the lids on the jars and screw on the bands until fingertip tight.
12. Process the filled jars in a boiling water canner for 10 minutes (adjust for altitude if necessary).
13. Remove the jars from the canner and let them cool completely at room temperature. Check the seals before storing.
14. Store the jars in a cool, dark place for up to a year. Once opened, store in the refrigerator and use within a few weeks.

This Tomato Basil Jam is perfect for spreading on toast, sandwiches, or crackers, or for using as a topping for grilled meats or vegetables. Enjoy the savory and herby flavors!

**Jalapeno Peach Jam**

Ingredients:

- 4 cups (about 900g) ripe peaches, peeled, pitted, and chopped
- 1 cup (200g) granulated sugar
- 1/2 cup (120ml) apple cider vinegar
- 2 jalapeno peppers, seeded and finely chopped
- Juice of 1 lemon
- Zest of 1 lemon
- Pinch of salt

Instructions:

1. Prepare your canning jars and lids according to proper canning procedures.
2. In a large, heavy-bottomed pot, combine the chopped peaches, sugar, apple cider vinegar, chopped jalapeno peppers, lemon juice, lemon zest, and a pinch of salt.
3. Stir the mixture well to combine.
4. Place the pot over medium-high heat and bring the mixture to a full rolling boil, stirring constantly.
5. Reduce the heat to medium-low and let the mixture simmer, stirring occasionally, until it thickens and reaches the desired consistency. This typically takes about 30-40 minutes.
6. To test if the jam is ready, place a small amount on a chilled plate and let it cool for a minute. If it wrinkles when you push it with your finger, it's ready.
7. Once the jam reaches the desired consistency, remove the pot from the heat.
8. Ladle the hot jam into prepared jars, leaving about 1/4 inch of headspace.
9. Wipe the rims of the jars with a clean, damp cloth to remove any residue.
10. Place the lids on the jars and screw on the bands until fingertip tight.
11. Process the filled jars in a boiling water canner for 10 minutes (adjust for altitude if necessary).
12. Remove the jars from the canner and let them cool completely at room temperature. Check the seals before storing.
13. Store the jars in a cool, dark place for up to a year. Once opened, store in the refrigerator and use within a few weeks.

This Jalapeno Peach Jam is perfect for spreading on toast, biscuits, or crackers, or for using as a glaze for grilled meats or seafood. Enjoy the sweet and spicy flavors!

**Raspberry Chipotle Jam**

Ingredients:

- 4 cups (about 600g) fresh raspberries
- 1 cup (200g) granulated sugar
- 2 chipotle peppers in adobo sauce, finely chopped
- Juice of 1 lime
- Zest of 1 lime

Instructions:

1. Prepare your canning jars and lids according to proper canning procedures.
2. In a large, heavy-bottomed pot, combine the raspberries, sugar, chopped chipotle peppers, lime juice, and lime zest.
3. Stir the mixture well to combine.
4. Place the pot over medium-high heat and bring the mixture to a full rolling boil, stirring constantly.
5. Reduce the heat to medium-low and let the mixture simmer, stirring occasionally, until it thickens and reaches the desired consistency. This typically takes about 20-30 minutes.
6. To test if the jam is ready, place a small amount on a chilled plate and let it cool for a minute. If it wrinkles when you push it with your finger, it's ready.
7. Once the jam reaches the desired consistency, remove the pot from the heat.
8. Ladle the hot jam into prepared jars, leaving about 1/4 inch of headspace.
9. Wipe the rims of the jars with a clean, damp cloth to remove any residue.
10. Place the lids on the jars and screw on the bands until fingertip tight.
11. Process the filled jars in a boiling water canner for 10 minutes (adjust for altitude if necessary).
12. Remove the jars from the canner and let them cool completely at room temperature. Check the seals before storing.
13. Store the jars in a cool, dark place for up to a year. Once opened, store in the refrigerator and use within a few weeks.

This Raspberry Chipotle Jam is perfect for spreading on toast, muffins, or scones, or for using as a glaze for grilled meats or vegetables. Enjoy the sweet and smoky flavors!

**Blueberry Lavender Jam**

Ingredients:

- 4 cups (about 600g) fresh blueberries
- 1 cup (200g) granulated sugar
- 2 tablespoons dried culinary lavender buds
- Juice and zest of 1 lemon

Instructions:

1. Prepare your canning jars and lids according to proper canning procedures.
2. In a large, heavy-bottomed pot, combine the blueberries, sugar, dried lavender buds, lemon juice, and lemon zest.
3. Stir the mixture well to combine.
4. Place the pot over medium-high heat and bring the mixture to a full rolling boil, stirring constantly.
5. Reduce the heat to medium-low and let the mixture simmer, stirring occasionally, until it thickens and reaches the desired consistency. This typically takes about 20-30 minutes.
6. To test if the jam is ready, place a small amount on a chilled plate and let it cool for a minute. If it wrinkles when you push it with your finger, it's ready.
7. Once the jam reaches the desired consistency, remove the pot from the heat.
8. If desired, strain the jam through a fine-mesh sieve to remove the lavender buds.
9. Ladle the hot jam into prepared jars, leaving about 1/4 inch of headspace.
10. Wipe the rims of the jars with a clean, damp cloth to remove any residue.
11. Place the lids on the jars and screw on the bands until fingertip tight.
12. Process the filled jars in a boiling water canner for 10 minutes (adjust for altitude if necessary).
13. Remove the jars from the canner and let them cool completely at room temperature. Check the seals before storing.
14. Store the jars in a cool, dark place for up to a year. Once opened, store in the refrigerator and use within a few weeks.

This Blueberry Lavender Jam is perfect for spreading on toast, pancakes, or yogurt, or for using as a filling in pastries or cakes. Enjoy the sweet and floral flavors!

**Strawberry Basil Jam**

Ingredients:

- 4 cups (about 600g) fresh strawberries, hulled and chopped
- 1 cup (200g) granulated sugar
- Juice and zest of 1 lemon
- 1/4 cup (10g) fresh basil leaves, chopped

Instructions:

1. Prepare your canning jars and lids according to proper canning procedures.
2. In a large, heavy-bottomed pot, combine the chopped strawberries, sugar, lemon juice, and lemon zest.
3. Stir the mixture well to combine.
4. Place the pot over medium-high heat and bring the mixture to a full rolling boil, stirring constantly.
5. Reduce the heat to medium-low and let the mixture simmer, stirring occasionally, until it thickens and reaches the desired consistency. This typically takes about 20-30 minutes.
6. To test if the jam is ready, place a small amount on a chilled plate and let it cool for a minute. If it wrinkles when you push it with your finger, it's ready.
7. Once the jam reaches the desired consistency, remove the pot from the heat.
8. Stir in the chopped basil leaves and let the jam cool for a few minutes.
9. Ladle the hot jam into prepared jars, leaving about 1/4 inch of headspace.
10. Wipe the rims of the jars with a clean, damp cloth to remove any residue.
11. Place the lids on the jars and screw on the bands until fingertip tight.
12. Process the filled jars in a boiling water canner for 10 minutes (adjust for altitude if necessary).
13. Remove the jars from the canner and let them cool completely at room temperature. Check the seals before storing.
14. Store the jars in a cool, dark place for up to a year. Once opened, store in the refrigerator and use within a few weeks.

This Strawberry Basil Jam is perfect for spreading on toast, muffins, or scones, or for using as a topping for yogurt or ice cream. Enjoy the sweet and herby flavors!

**Cranberry Jalapeno Jam**

Ingredients:

- 12 ounces (about 340g) fresh cranberries
- 2-3 jalapeno peppers, seeded and finely chopped
- 1 cup (200g) granulated sugar
- 1/2 cup (120ml) water
- Juice and zest of 1 lime
- Pinch of salt

Instructions:

1. In a medium saucepan, combine the cranberries, chopped jalapeno peppers, sugar, water, lime juice, lime zest, and a pinch of salt.
2. Place the saucepan over medium-high heat and bring the mixture to a boil.
3. Reduce the heat to medium-low and let the mixture simmer, stirring occasionally, until the cranberries burst and the mixture thickens, about 15-20 minutes.
4. Use a potato masher or the back of a spoon to mash any remaining whole cranberries and jalapeno pieces.
5. Continue to cook the jam for another 5-10 minutes, or until it reaches your desired consistency.
6. Remove the saucepan from the heat and let the jam cool for a few minutes.
7. Transfer the jam to clean, sterilized jars.
8. Let the jam cool completely before sealing the jars.
9. Store the jars in the refrigerator for up to 2 weeks.

This Cranberry Jalapeno Jam is perfect for serving with cheese and crackers, as a glaze for meats, or as a condiment for sandwiches or burgers. Enjoy the sweet and spicy flavors!

**Ginger Pear Jam**

Ingredients:

- 4 cups (about 900g) ripe pears, peeled, cored, and diced
- 1 cup (200g) granulated sugar
- 2 tablespoons fresh ginger, peeled and grated
- Juice and zest of 1 lemon
- 1/4 teaspoon ground cinnamon (optional)

Instructions:

1. Prepare your canning jars and lids according to proper canning procedures.
2. In a large, heavy-bottomed pot, combine the diced pears, sugar, grated ginger, lemon juice, lemon zest, and ground cinnamon (if using).
3. Stir the mixture well to combine.
4. Place the pot over medium-high heat and bring the mixture to a full rolling boil, stirring constantly.
5. Reduce the heat to medium-low and let the mixture simmer, stirring occasionally, until it thickens and reaches the desired consistency. This typically takes about 30-40 minutes.
6. To test if the jam is ready, place a small amount on a chilled plate and let it cool for a minute. If it wrinkles when you push it with your finger, it's ready.
7. Once the jam reaches the desired consistency, remove the pot from the heat.
8. Ladle the hot jam into prepared jars, leaving about 1/4 inch of headspace.
9. Wipe the rims of the jars with a clean, damp cloth to remove any residue.
10. Place the lids on the jars and screw on the bands until fingertip tight.
11. Process the filled jars in a boiling water canner for 10 minutes (adjust for altitude if necessary).
12. Remove the jars from the canner and let them cool completely at room temperature. Check the seals before storing.
13. Store the jars in a cool, dark place for up to a year. Once opened, store in the refrigerator and use within a few weeks.

This Ginger Pear Jam is perfect for spreading on toast, biscuits, or scones, or for using as a filling in pastries or thumbprint cookies. Enjoy the sweet and spicy flavors!

**Pineapple Coconut Jam**

Ingredients:

- 4 cups (about 600g) fresh pineapple, finely chopped
- 1 cup (200g) granulated sugar
- 1 cup (240ml) coconut milk
- Juice and zest of 1 lime
- 1/2 cup (40g) shredded coconut

Instructions:

1. In a large, heavy-bottomed pot, combine the chopped pineapple, sugar, coconut milk, lime juice, and lime zest.
2. Stir the mixture well to combine.
3. Place the pot over medium-high heat and bring the mixture to a boil, stirring constantly.
4. Reduce the heat to medium-low and let the mixture simmer, stirring occasionally, until it thickens and reaches the desired consistency. This typically takes about 30-40 minutes.
5. Stir in the shredded coconut and continue to cook for another 5 minutes.
6. To test if the jam is ready, place a small amount on a chilled plate and let it cool for a minute. If it wrinkles when you push it with your finger, it's ready.
7. Once the jam reaches the desired consistency, remove the pot from the heat.
8. Ladle the hot jam into prepared jars, leaving about 1/4 inch of headspace.
9. Wipe the rims of the jars with a clean, damp cloth to remove any residue.
10. Place the lids on the jars and screw on the bands until fingertip tight.
11. Process the filled jars in a boiling water canner for 10 minutes (adjust for altitude if necessary).
12. Remove the jars from the canner and let them cool completely at room temperature. Check the seals before storing.
13. Store the jars in a cool, dark place for up to a year. Once opened, store in the refrigerator and use within a few weeks.

This Pineapple Coconut Jam is perfect for spreading on toast, muffins, or pancakes, or for using as a filling in cakes or pastries. Enjoy the tropical flavors!

**Apricot Rosemary Jam**

Ingredients:

- 4 cups (about 900g) ripe apricots, pitted and chopped
- 1 cup (200g) granulated sugar
- Juice and zest of 1 lemon
- 2 tablespoons fresh rosemary leaves, chopped finely

Instructions:

1. Prepare your canning jars and lids according to proper canning procedures.
2. In a large, heavy-bottomed pot, combine the chopped apricots, sugar, lemon juice, lemon zest, and chopped rosemary leaves.
3. Stir the mixture well to combine.
4. Place the pot over medium-high heat and bring the mixture to a full rolling boil, stirring constantly.
5. Reduce the heat to medium-low and let the mixture simmer, stirring occasionally, until it thickens and reaches the desired consistency. This typically takes about 20-30 minutes.
6. To test if the jam is ready, place a small amount on a chilled plate and let it cool for a minute. If it wrinkles when you push it with your finger, it's ready.
7. Once the jam reaches the desired consistency, remove the pot from the heat.
8. Ladle the hot jam into prepared jars, leaving about 1/4 inch of headspace.
9. Wipe the rims of the jars with a clean, damp cloth to remove any residue.
10. Place the lids on the jars and screw on the bands until fingertip tight.
11. Process the filled jars in a boiling water canner for 10 minutes (adjust for altitude if necessary).
12. Remove the jars from the canner and let them cool completely at room temperature. Check the seals before storing.
13. Store the jars in a cool, dark place for up to a year. Once opened, store in the refrigerator and use within a few weeks.

This Apricot Rosemary Jam is perfect for spreading on toast, scones, or crackers, or for using as a glaze for meats or roasted vegetables. Enjoy the sweet and herby flavors!

**Mango Habanero Jam**

Ingredients:

- 4 cups (about 900g) ripe mangoes, peeled, pitted, and diced
- 1 cup (200g) granulated sugar
- Juice and zest of 1 lime
- 2-3 habanero peppers, seeded and finely chopped (adjust to taste)
- 1 teaspoon grated fresh ginger
- Pinch of salt

Instructions:

1. Prepare your canning jars and lids according to proper canning procedures.
2. In a large, heavy-bottomed pot, combine the diced mangoes, sugar, lime juice, lime zest, chopped habanero peppers, grated ginger, and a pinch of salt.
3. Stir the mixture well to combine.
4. Place the pot over medium-high heat and bring the mixture to a full rolling boil, stirring constantly.
5. Reduce the heat to medium-low and let the mixture simmer, stirring occasionally, until it thickens and reaches the desired consistency. This typically takes about 30-40 minutes.
6. To test if the jam is ready, place a small amount on a chilled plate and let it cool for a minute. If it wrinkles when you push it with your finger, it's ready.
7. Once the jam reaches the desired consistency, remove the pot from the heat.
8. Ladle the hot jam into prepared jars, leaving about 1/4 inch of headspace.
9. Wipe the rims of the jars with a clean, damp cloth to remove any residue.
10. Place the lids on the jars and screw on the bands until fingertip tight.
11. Process the filled jars in a boiling water canner for 10 minutes (adjust for altitude if necessary).
12. Remove the jars from the canner and let them cool completely at room temperature. Check the seals before storing.
13. Store the jars in a cool, dark place for up to a year. Once opened, store in the refrigerator and use within a few weeks.

This Mango Habanero Jam is perfect for spreading on toast, sandwiches, or crackers, or for using as a glaze for grilled meats or seafood. Enjoy the sweet and spicy flavors!

**Peach Thyme Jam**

Ingredients:

- 4 cups (about 900g) ripe peaches, peeled, pitted, and chopped
- 1 cup (200g) granulated sugar
- Juice and zest of 1 lemon
- 2-3 sprigs of fresh thyme, leaves removed and chopped finely
- Pinch of salt

Instructions:

1. Prepare your canning jars and lids according to proper canning procedures.
2. In a large, heavy-bottomed pot, combine the chopped peaches, sugar, lemon juice, lemon zest, chopped thyme leaves, and a pinch of salt.
3. Stir the mixture well to combine.
4. Place the pot over medium-high heat and bring the mixture to a full rolling boil, stirring constantly.
5. Reduce the heat to medium-low and let the mixture simmer, stirring occasionally, until it thickens and reaches the desired consistency. This typically takes about 20-30 minutes.
6. To test if the jam is ready, place a small amount on a chilled plate and let it cool for a minute. If it wrinkles when you push it with your finger, it's ready.
7. Once the jam reaches the desired consistency, remove the pot from the heat.
8. Ladle the hot jam into prepared jars, leaving about 1/4 inch of headspace.
9. Wipe the rims of the jars with a clean, damp cloth to remove any residue.
10. Place the lids on the jars and screw on the bands until fingertip tight.
11. Process the filled jars in a boiling water canner for 10 minutes (adjust for altitude if necessary).
12. Remove the jars from the canner and let them cool completely at room temperature. Check the seals before storing.
13. Store the jars in a cool, dark place for up to a year. Once opened, store in the refrigerator and use within a few weeks.

This Peach Thyme Jam is perfect for spreading on toast, biscuits, or scones, or for using as a filling in pastries or thumbprint cookies. Enjoy the sweet and herby flavors!

**Blackberry Lemon Thyme Jam**

Ingredients:

- 4 cups (about 600g) fresh blackberries
- 1 cup (200g) granulated sugar
- Juice and zest of 2 lemons
- 2-3 sprigs of fresh thyme, leaves removed and chopped finely

Instructions:

1. Prepare your canning jars and lids according to proper canning procedures.
2. In a large, heavy-bottomed pot, combine the blackberries, sugar, lemon juice, lemon zest, and chopped thyme leaves.
3. Stir the mixture well to combine.
4. Place the pot over medium-high heat and bring the mixture to a full rolling boil, stirring constantly.
5. Reduce the heat to medium-low and let the mixture simmer, stirring occasionally, until it thickens and reaches the desired consistency. This typically takes about 20-30 minutes.
6. To test if the jam is ready, place a small amount on a chilled plate and let it cool for a minute. If it wrinkles when you push it with your finger, it's ready.
7. Once the jam reaches the desired consistency, remove the pot from the heat.
8. Ladle the hot jam into prepared jars, leaving about 1/4 inch of headspace.
9. Wipe the rims of the jars with a clean, damp cloth to remove any residue.
10. Place the lids on the jars and screw on the bands until fingertip tight.
11. Process the filled jars in a boiling water canner for 10 minutes (adjust for altitude if necessary).
12. Remove the jars from the canner and let them cool completely at room temperature. Check the seals before storing.
13. Store the jars in a cool, dark place for up to a year. Once opened, store in the refrigerator and use within a few weeks.

This Blackberry Lemon Thyme Jam is perfect for spreading on toast, scones, or muffins, or for using as a filling in cakes or pastries. Enjoy the sweet and herby flavors!

**Raspberry Vanilla Bean Jam**

Ingredients:

- 4 cups (about 600g) fresh raspberries
- 1 cup (200g) granulated sugar
- Juice and zest of 1 lemon
- 1 vanilla bean pod, split lengthwise and seeds scraped out

Instructions:

1. Prepare your canning jars and lids according to proper canning procedures.
2. In a large, heavy-bottomed pot, combine the raspberries, sugar, lemon juice, lemon zest, and scraped vanilla bean seeds. Place the empty vanilla bean pod into the mixture as well.
3. Stir the mixture well to combine.
4. Place the pot over medium-high heat and bring the mixture to a full rolling boil, stirring constantly.
5. Reduce the heat to medium-low and let the mixture simmer, stirring occasionally, until it thickens and reaches the desired consistency. This typically takes about 20-30 minutes.
6. To test if the jam is ready, place a small amount on a chilled plate and let it cool for a minute. If it wrinkles when you push it with your finger, it's ready.
7. Once the jam reaches the desired consistency, remove the pot from the heat and discard the vanilla bean pod.
8. Ladle the hot jam into prepared jars, leaving about 1/4 inch of headspace.
9. Wipe the rims of the jars with a clean, damp cloth to remove any residue.
10. Place the lids on the jars and screw on the bands until fingertip tight.
11. Process the filled jars in a boiling water canner for 10 minutes (adjust for altitude if necessary).
12. Remove the jars from the canner and let them cool completely at room temperature. Check the seals before storing.
13. Store the jars in a cool, dark place for up to a year. Once opened, store in the refrigerator and use within a few weeks.

This Raspberry Vanilla Bean Jam is perfect for spreading on toast, scones, or pancakes, or for using as a filling in cakes or pastries. Enjoy the sweet and aromatic flavors!

**Cherry Lime Jam**

Ingredients:

- 4 cups (about 600g) fresh cherries, pitted and chopped
- 1 cup (200g) granulated sugar
- Juice and zest of 2 limes

Instructions:

1. Prepare your canning jars and lids according to proper canning procedures.
2. In a large, heavy-bottomed pot, combine the chopped cherries, sugar, lime juice, and lime zest.
3. Stir the mixture well to combine.
4. Place the pot over medium-high heat and bring the mixture to a full rolling boil, stirring constantly.
5. Reduce the heat to medium-low and let the mixture simmer, stirring occasionally, until it thickens and reaches the desired consistency. This typically takes about 20-30 minutes.
6. To test if the jam is ready, place a small amount on a chilled plate and let it cool for a minute. If it wrinkles when you push it with your finger, it's ready.
7. Once the jam reaches the desired consistency, remove the pot from the heat.
8. Ladle the hot jam into prepared jars, leaving about 1/4 inch of headspace.
9. Wipe the rims of the jars with a clean, damp cloth to remove any residue.
10. Place the lids on the jars and screw on the bands until fingertip tight.
11. Process the filled jars in a boiling water canner for 10 minutes (adjust for altitude if necessary).
12. Remove the jars from the canner and let them cool completely at room temperature. Check the seals before storing.
13. Store the jars in a cool, dark place for up to a year. Once opened, store in the refrigerator and use within a few weeks.

This Cherry Lime Jam is perfect for spreading on toast, muffins, or scones, or for using as a filling in cakes or pastries. Enjoy the sweet and tangy flavors!

**Grapefruit Rose Jam**

Ingredients:

- 4 cups (about 900g) grapefruit, peeled, seeded, and chopped
- 1 cup (200g) granulated sugar
- Juice and zest of 1 lemon
- 2-3 teaspoons dried rose petals, finely chopped

Instructions:

1. Prepare your canning jars and lids according to proper canning procedures.
2. In a large, heavy-bottomed pot, combine the chopped grapefruit, sugar, lemon juice, lemon zest, and chopped dried rose petals.
3. Stir the mixture well to combine.
4. Place the pot over medium-high heat and bring the mixture to a full rolling boil, stirring constantly.
5. Reduce the heat to medium-low and let the mixture simmer, stirring occasionally, until it thickens and reaches the desired consistency. This typically takes about 30-40 minutes.
6. To test if the jam is ready, place a small amount on a chilled plate and let it cool for a minute. If it wrinkles when you push it with your finger, it's ready.
7. Once the jam reaches the desired consistency, remove the pot from the heat.
8. Ladle the hot jam into prepared jars, leaving about 1/4 inch of headspace.
9. Wipe the rims of the jars with a clean, damp cloth to remove any residue.
10. Place the lids on the jars and screw on the bands until fingertip tight.
11. Process the filled jars in a boiling water canner for 10 minutes (adjust for altitude if necessary).
12. Remove the jars from the canner and let them cool completely at room temperature. Check the seals before storing.
13. Store the jars in a cool, dark place for up to a year. Once opened, store in the refrigerator and use within a few weeks.

This Grapefruit Rose Jam is perfect for spreading on toast, scones, or crackers, or for using as a filling in cakes or pastries. Enjoy the citrusy and floral flavors!

**Pear Cardamom Jam**

Ingredients:

- 4 cups (about 900g) ripe pears, peeled, cored, and chopped
- 1 cup (200g) granulated sugar
- Juice and zest of 1 lemon
- 1 teaspoon ground cardamom
- Pinch of salt

Instructions:

1. Prepare your canning jars and lids according to proper canning procedures.
2. In a large, heavy-bottomed pot, combine the chopped pears, sugar, lemon juice, lemon zest, ground cardamom, and a pinch of salt.
3. Stir the mixture well to combine.
4. Place the pot over medium-high heat and bring the mixture to a full rolling boil, stirring constantly.
5. Reduce the heat to medium-low and let the mixture simmer, stirring occasionally, until it thickens and reaches the desired consistency. This typically takes about 20-30 minutes.
6. To test if the jam is ready, place a small amount on a chilled plate and let it cool for a minute. If it wrinkles when you push it with your finger, it's ready.
7. Once the jam reaches the desired consistency, remove the pot from the heat.
8. Ladle the hot jam into prepared jars, leaving about 1/4 inch of headspace.
9. Wipe the rims of the jars with a clean, damp cloth to remove any residue.
10. Place the lids on the jars and screw on the bands until fingertip tight.
11. Process the filled jars in a boiling water canner for 10 minutes (adjust for altitude if necessary).
12. Remove the jars from the canner and let them cool completely at room temperature. Check the seals before storing.
13. Store the jars in a cool, dark place for up to a year. Once opened, store in the refrigerator and use within a few weeks.

This Pear Cardamom Jam is perfect for spreading on toast, scones, or biscuits, or for using as a filling in pastries or thumbprint cookies. Enjoy the sweet and aromatic flavors!

**Strawberry Mint Jam**

Ingredients:

- 4 cups (about 600g) fresh strawberries, hulled and chopped
- 1 cup (200g) granulated sugar
- Juice and zest of 1 lemon
- 1/4 cup (about 10g) fresh mint leaves, chopped finely

Instructions:

1. Prepare your canning jars and lids according to proper canning procedures.
2. In a large, heavy-bottomed pot, combine the chopped strawberries, sugar, lemon juice, lemon zest, and chopped mint leaves.
3. Stir the mixture well to combine.
4. Place the pot over medium-high heat and bring the mixture to a full rolling boil, stirring constantly.
5. Reduce the heat to medium-low and let the mixture simmer, stirring occasionally, until it thickens and reaches the desired consistency. This typically takes about 20-30 minutes.
6. To test if the jam is ready, place a small amount on a chilled plate and let it cool for a minute. If it wrinkles when you push it with your finger, it's ready.
7. Once the jam reaches the desired consistency, remove the pot from the heat.
8. Ladle the hot jam into prepared jars, leaving about 1/4 inch of headspace.
9. Wipe the rims of the jars with a clean, damp cloth to remove any residue.
10. Place the lids on the jars and screw on the bands until fingertip tight.
11. Process the filled jars in a boiling water canner for 10 minutes (adjust for altitude if necessary).
12. Remove the jars from the canner and let them cool completely at room temperature. Check the seals before storing.
13. Store the jars in a cool, dark place for up to a year. Once opened, store in the refrigerator and use within a few weeks.

This Strawberry Mint Jam is perfect for spreading on toast, scones, or pancakes, or for using as a filling in cakes or pastries. Enjoy the sweet and refreshing flavors!

**Blueberry Lime Jam**

Ingredients:

- 4 cups (about 600g) fresh blueberries
- 1 cup (200g) granulated sugar
- Juice and zest of 2 limes

Instructions:

1. Prepare your canning jars and lids according to proper canning procedures.
2. In a large, heavy-bottomed pot, combine the blueberries, sugar, lime juice, and lime zest.
3. Stir the mixture well to combine.
4. Place the pot over medium-high heat and bring the mixture to a full rolling boil, stirring constantly.
5. Reduce the heat to medium-low and let the mixture simmer, stirring occasionally, until it thickens and reaches the desired consistency. This typically takes about 20-30 minutes.
6. To test if the jam is ready, place a small amount on a chilled plate and let it cool for a minute. If it wrinkles when you push it with your finger, it's ready.
7. Once the jam reaches the desired consistency, remove the pot from the heat.
8. Ladle the hot jam into prepared jars, leaving about 1/4 inch of headspace.
9. Wipe the rims of the jars with a clean, damp cloth to remove any residue.
10. Place the lids on the jars and screw on the bands until fingertip tight.
11. Process the filled jars in a boiling water canner for 10 minutes (adjust for altitude if necessary).
12. Remove the jars from the canner and let them cool completely at room temperature. Check the seals before storing.
13. Store the jars in a cool, dark place for up to a year. Once opened, store in the refrigerator and use within a few weeks.

This Blueberry Lime Jam is perfect for spreading on toast, muffins, or scones, or for using as a filling in cakes or pastries. Enjoy the sweet and tangy flavors!

**Pineapple Mango Jam**

Ingredients:

- 2 cups (about 300g) diced fresh pineapple
- 2 cups (about 300g) diced ripe mango
- 1 cup (200g) granulated sugar
- Juice and zest of 1 lime

Instructions:

1. Prepare your canning jars and lids according to proper canning procedures.
2. In a large, heavy-bottomed pot, combine the diced pineapple, diced mango, sugar, lime juice, and lime zest.
3. Stir the mixture well to combine.
4. Place the pot over medium-high heat and bring the mixture to a full rolling boil, stirring constantly.
5. Reduce the heat to medium-low and let the mixture simmer, stirring occasionally, until it thickens and reaches the desired consistency. This typically takes about 20-30 minutes.
6. To test if the jam is ready, place a small amount on a chilled plate and let it cool for a minute. If it wrinkles when you push it with your finger, it's ready.
7. Once the jam reaches the desired consistency, remove the pot from the heat.
8. Ladle the hot jam into prepared jars, leaving about 1/4 inch of headspace.
9. Wipe the rims of the jars with a clean, damp cloth to remove any residue.
10. Place the lids on the jars and screw on the bands until fingertip tight.
11. Process the filled jars in a boiling water canner for 10 minutes (adjust for altitude if necessary).
12. Remove the jars from the canner and let them cool completely at room temperature. Check the seals before storing.
13. Store the jars in a cool, dark place for up to a year. Once opened, store in the refrigerator and use within a few weeks.

This Pineapple Mango Jam is perfect for spreading on toast, pancakes, or waffles, or for using as a filling in pastries or thumbprint cookies. Enjoy the tropical flavors!

**Peach Jalapeno Jam**

Ingredients:

- 4 cups (about 600g) ripe peaches, peeled, pitted, and chopped
- 2-3 jalapeño peppers, seeded and finely chopped
- 1 cup (200g) granulated sugar
- Juice and zest of 1 lime

Instructions:

1. Prepare your canning jars and lids according to proper canning procedures.
2. In a large, heavy-bottomed pot, combine the chopped peaches, chopped jalapeño peppers, sugar, lime juice, and lime zest.
3. Stir the mixture well to combine.
4. Place the pot over medium-high heat and bring the mixture to a full rolling boil, stirring constantly.
5. Reduce the heat to medium-low and let the mixture simmer, stirring occasionally, until it thickens and reaches the desired consistency. This typically takes about 20-30 minutes.
6. To test if the jam is ready, place a small amount on a chilled plate and let it cool for a minute. If it wrinkles when you push it with your finger, it's ready.
7. Once the jam reaches the desired consistency, remove the pot from the heat.
8. Ladle the hot jam into prepared jars, leaving about 1/4 inch of headspace.
9. Wipe the rims of the jars with a clean, damp cloth to remove any residue.
10. Place the lids on the jars and screw on the bands until fingertip tight.
11. Process the filled jars in a boiling water canner for 10 minutes (adjust for altitude if necessary).
12. Remove the jars from the canner and let them cool completely at room temperature. Check the seals before storing.
13. Store the jars in a cool, dark place for up to a year. Once opened, store in the refrigerator and use within a few weeks.

This Peach Jalapeño Jam is perfect for spreading on toast, sandwiches, or crackers, or for using as a glaze for meats or roasted vegetables. Enjoy the sweet and spicy flavors!

**Tomato Peach Jam**

Ingredients:

- 4 cups (about 600g) ripe tomatoes, peeled, seeded, and chopped
- 2 cups (about 300g) ripe peaches, peeled, pitted, and chopped
- 1 cup (200g) granulated sugar
- Juice and zest of 1 lemon
- 1 teaspoon ground cinnamon (optional)
- Pinch of salt

Instructions:

1. Prepare your canning jars and lids according to proper canning procedures.
2. In a large, heavy-bottomed pot, combine the chopped tomatoes, chopped peaches, sugar, lemon juice, lemon zest, ground cinnamon (if using), and a pinch of salt.
3. Stir the mixture well to combine.
4. Place the pot over medium-high heat and bring the mixture to a full rolling boil, stirring constantly.
5. Reduce the heat to medium-low and let the mixture simmer, stirring occasionally, until it thickens and reaches the desired consistency. This typically takes about 30-40 minutes.
6. To test if the jam is ready, place a small amount on a chilled plate and let it cool for a minute. If it wrinkles when you push it with your finger, it's ready.
7. Once the jam reaches the desired consistency, remove the pot from the heat.
8. Ladle the hot jam into prepared jars, leaving about 1/4 inch of headspace.
9. Wipe the rims of the jars with a clean, damp cloth to remove any residue.
10. Place the lids on the jars and screw on the bands until fingertip tight.
11. Process the filled jars in a boiling water canner for 10 minutes (adjust for altitude if necessary).
12. Remove the jars from the canner and let them cool completely at room temperature. Check the seals before storing.
13. Store the jars in a cool, dark place for up to a year. Once opened, store in the refrigerator and use within a few weeks.

This Tomato Peach Jam is perfect for spreading on toast, sandwiches, or crackers, or for using as a topping for grilled meats or fish. Enjoy the sweet and savory flavors!

**Raspberry Jalapeno Jam**

Ingredients:

- 4 cups (about 600g) fresh raspberries
- 2-3 jalapeño peppers, seeded and finely chopped
- 1 cup (200g) granulated sugar
- Juice and zest of 1 lime

Instructions:

1. Prepare your canning jars and lids according to proper canning procedures.
2. In a large, heavy-bottomed pot, combine the raspberries, chopped jalapeño peppers, sugar, lime juice, and lime zest.
3. Stir the mixture well to combine.
4. Place the pot over medium-high heat and bring the mixture to a full rolling boil, stirring constantly.
5. Reduce the heat to medium-low and let the mixture simmer, stirring occasionally, until it thickens and reaches the desired consistency. This typically takes about 20-30 minutes.
6. To test if the jam is ready, place a small amount on a chilled plate and let it cool for a minute. If it wrinkles when you push it with your finger, it's ready.
7. Once the jam reaches the desired consistency, remove the pot from the heat.
8. Ladle the hot jam into prepared jars, leaving about 1/4 inch of headspace.
9. Wipe the rims of the jars with a clean, damp cloth to remove any residue.
10. Place the lids on the jars and screw on the bands until fingertip tight.
11. Process the filled jars in a boiling water canner for 10 minutes (adjust for altitude if necessary).
12. Remove the jars from the canner and let them cool completely at room temperature. Check the seals before storing.
13. Store the jars in a cool, dark place for up to a year. Once opened, store in the refrigerator and use within a few weeks.

This Raspberry Jalapeño Jam is perfect for spreading on toast, muffins, or scones, or for using as a glaze for meats or roasted vegetables. Enjoy the sweet and spicy flavors!

**Strawberry Rhubarb Ginger Jam**

Ingredients:

- 2 cups (about 300g) diced fresh rhubarb
- 2 cups (about 300g) sliced fresh strawberries
- 1 cup (200g) granulated sugar
- Juice and zest of 1 lemon
- 1 tablespoon grated fresh ginger

Instructions:

1. Prepare your canning jars and lids according to proper canning procedures.
2. In a large, heavy-bottomed pot, combine the diced rhubarb, sliced strawberries, sugar, lemon juice, lemon zest, and grated ginger.
3. Stir the mixture well to combine.
4. Place the pot over medium-high heat and bring the mixture to a full rolling boil, stirring constantly.
5. Reduce the heat to medium-low and let the mixture simmer, stirring occasionally, until it thickens and reaches the desired consistency. This typically takes about 20-30 minutes.
6. To test if the jam is ready, place a small amount on a chilled plate and let it cool for a minute. If it wrinkles when you push it with your finger, it's ready.
7. Once the jam reaches the desired consistency, remove the pot from the heat.
8. Ladle the hot jam into prepared jars, leaving about 1/4 inch of headspace.
9. Wipe the rims of the jars with a clean, damp cloth to remove any residue.
10. Place the lids on the jars and screw on the bands until fingertip tight.
11. Process the filled jars in a boiling water canner for 10 minutes (adjust for altitude if necessary).
12. Remove the jars from the canner and let them cool completely at room temperature. Check the seals before storing.
13. Store the jars in a cool, dark place for up to a year. Once opened, store in the refrigerator and use within a few weeks.

This Strawberry Rhubarb Ginger Jam is perfect for spreading on toast, scones, or biscuits, or for using as a filling in cakes or pastries. Enjoy the sweet and tangy flavors with a hint of ginger!

**Apple Cinnamon Jam**

Ingredients:

- 4 cups (about 600g) apples, peeled, cored, and chopped
- 1 cup (200g) granulated sugar
- Juice and zest of 1 lemon
- 2 teaspoons ground cinnamon
- Pinch of salt

Instructions:

1. Prepare your canning jars and lids according to proper canning procedures.
2. In a large, heavy-bottomed pot, combine the chopped apples, sugar, lemon juice, lemon zest, ground cinnamon, and a pinch of salt.
3. Stir the mixture well to combine.
4. Place the pot over medium-high heat and bring the mixture to a full rolling boil, stirring constantly.
5. Reduce the heat to medium-low and let the mixture simmer, stirring occasionally, until it thickens and reaches the desired consistency. This typically takes about 20-30 minutes.
6. To test if the jam is ready, place a small amount on a chilled plate and let it cool for a minute. If it wrinkles when you push it with your finger, it's ready.
7. Once the jam reaches the desired consistency, remove the pot from the heat.
8. Ladle the hot jam into prepared jars, leaving about 1/4 inch of headspace.
9. Wipe the rims of the jars with a clean, damp cloth to remove any residue.
10. Place the lids on the jars and screw on the bands until fingertip tight.
11. Process the filled jars in a boiling water canner for 10 minutes (adjust for altitude if necessary).
12. Remove the jars from the canner and let them cool completely at room temperature. Check the seals before storing.
13. Store the jars in a cool, dark place for up to a year. Once opened, store in the refrigerator and use within a few weeks.

This Apple Cinnamon Jam is perfect for spreading on toast, muffins, or pancakes, or for using as a filling in cakes or pastries. Enjoy the cozy flavors of apple and cinnamon!

**Plum Port Jam**

Ingredients:

- 4 cups (about 600g) ripe plums, pitted and chopped
- 1 cup (200g) granulated sugar
- 1/2 cup (120ml) port wine
- Juice and zest of 1 lemon
- Pinch of salt

Instructions:

1. Prepare your canning jars and lids according to proper canning procedures.
2. In a large, heavy-bottomed pot, combine the chopped plums, sugar, port wine, lemon juice, lemon zest, and a pinch of salt.
3. Stir the mixture well to combine.
4. Place the pot over medium-high heat and bring the mixture to a full rolling boil, stirring constantly.
5. Reduce the heat to medium-low and let the mixture simmer, stirring occasionally, until it thickens and reaches the desired consistency. This typically takes about 30-40 minutes.
6. To test if the jam is ready, place a small amount on a chilled plate and let it cool for a minute. If it wrinkles when you push it with your finger, it's ready.
7. Once the jam reaches the desired consistency, remove the pot from the heat.
8. Ladle the hot jam into prepared jars, leaving about 1/4 inch of headspace.
9. Wipe the rims of the jars with a clean, damp cloth to remove any residue.
10. Place the lids on the jars and screw on the bands until fingertip tight.
11. Process the filled jars in a boiling water canner for 10 minutes (adjust for altitude if necessary).
12. Remove the jars from the canner and let them cool completely at room temperature. Check the seals before storing.
13. Store the jars in a cool, dark place for up to a year. Once opened, store in the refrigerator and use within a few weeks.

This Plum Port Jam is perfect for spreading on toast, scones, or muffins, or for using as a filling in cakes or pastries. Enjoy the rich and fruity flavors with a hint of port wine!

**Blueberry Lemon Verbena Jam**

Ingredients:

- 4 cups (about 600g) fresh blueberries
- 1 cup (200g) granulated sugar
- Juice and zest of 2 lemons
- 2 tablespoons chopped fresh lemon verbena leaves

Instructions:

1. Prepare your canning jars and lids according to proper canning procedures.
2. In a large, heavy-bottomed pot, combine the blueberries, sugar, lemon juice, lemon zest, and chopped lemon verbena leaves.
3. Stir the mixture well to combine.
4. Place the pot over medium-high heat and bring the mixture to a full rolling boil, stirring constantly.
5. Reduce the heat to medium-low and let the mixture simmer, stirring occasionally, until it thickens and reaches the desired consistency. This typically takes about 20-30 minutes.
6. To test if the jam is ready, place a small amount on a chilled plate and let it cool for a minute. If it wrinkles when you push it with your finger, it's ready.
7. Once the jam reaches the desired consistency, remove the pot from the heat.
8. Ladle the hot jam into prepared jars, leaving about 1/4 inch of headspace.
9. Wipe the rims of the jars with a clean, damp cloth to remove any residue.
10. Place the lids on the jars and screw on the bands until fingertip tight.
11. Process the filled jars in a boiling water canner for 10 minutes (adjust for altitude if necessary).
12. Remove the jars from the canner and let them cool completely at room temperature. Check the seals before storing.
13. Store the jars in a cool, dark place for up to a year. Once opened, store in the refrigerator and use within a few weeks.

This Blueberry Lemon Verbena Jam is perfect for spreading on toast, scones, or muffins, or for using as a topping for yogurt or ice cream. Enjoy the bright and citrusy flavors with a hint of herbal freshness from the lemon verbena!

**Peach Basil Jam**

Ingredients:

- 4 cups (about 600g) ripe peaches, peeled, pitted, and chopped
- 1 cup (200g) granulated sugar
- Juice and zest of 1 lemon
- 2 tablespoons chopped fresh basil leaves

Instructions:

1. Prepare your canning jars and lids according to proper canning procedures.
2. In a large, heavy-bottomed pot, combine the chopped peaches, sugar, lemon juice, lemon zest, and chopped basil leaves.
3. Stir the mixture well to combine.
4. Place the pot over medium-high heat and bring the mixture to a full rolling boil, stirring constantly.
5. Reduce the heat to medium-low and let the mixture simmer, stirring occasionally, until it thickens and reaches the desired consistency. This typically takes about 20-30 minutes.
6. To test if the jam is ready, place a small amount on a chilled plate and let it cool for a minute. If it wrinkles when you push it with your finger, it's ready.
7. Once the jam reaches the desired consistency, remove the pot from the heat.
8. Ladle the hot jam into prepared jars, leaving about 1/4 inch of headspace.
9. Wipe the rims of the jars with a clean, damp cloth to remove any residue.
10. Place the lids on the jars and screw on the bands until fingertip tight.
11. Process the filled jars in a boiling water canner for 10 minutes (adjust for altitude if necessary).
12. Remove the jars from the canner and let them cool completely at room temperature. Check the seals before storing.
13. Store the jars in a cool, dark place for up to a year. Once opened, store in the refrigerator and use within a few weeks.

This Peach Basil Jam is perfect for spreading on toast, scones, or biscuits, or for using as a filling in cakes or pastries. Enjoy the sweet and herbal flavors!

**Cherry Bourbon Jam**

Ingredients:

- 4 cups (about 600g) fresh cherries, pitted and chopped
- 1 cup (200g) granulated sugar
- Juice and zest of 1 lemon
- 1/4 cup (60ml) bourbon

Instructions:

1. Prepare your canning jars and lids according to proper canning procedures.
2. In a large, heavy-bottomed pot, combine the chopped cherries, sugar, lemon juice, lemon zest, and bourbon.
3. Stir the mixture well to combine.
4. Place the pot over medium-high heat and bring the mixture to a full rolling boil, stirring constantly.
5. Reduce the heat to medium-low and let the mixture simmer, stirring occasionally, until it thickens and reaches the desired consistency. This typically takes about 20-30 minutes.
6. To test if the jam is ready, place a small amount on a chilled plate and let it cool for a minute. If it wrinkles when you push it with your finger, it's ready.
7. Once the jam reaches the desired consistency, remove the pot from the heat.
8. Ladle the hot jam into prepared jars, leaving about 1/4 inch of headspace.
9. Wipe the rims of the jars with a clean, damp cloth to remove any residue.
10. Place the lids on the jars and screw on the bands until fingertip tight.
11. Process the filled jars in a boiling water canner for 10 minutes (adjust for altitude if necessary).
12. Remove the jars from the canner and let them cool completely at room temperature. Check the seals before storing.
13. Store the jars in a cool, dark place for up to a year. Once opened, store in the refrigerator and use within a few weeks.

This Cherry Bourbon Jam is perfect for spreading on toast, biscuits, or pancakes, or for using as a topping for yogurt or ice cream. Enjoy the rich and fruity flavors with a hint of bourbon!

**Strawberry Coconut Jam**

Ingredients:

- 4 cups (about 600g) fresh strawberries, hulled and chopped
- 1 cup (200g) granulated sugar
- Juice and zest of 1 lime
- 1 cup (240ml) coconut milk
- 1 teaspoon vanilla extract

Instructions:

1. Prepare your canning jars and lids according to proper canning procedures.
2. In a large, heavy-bottomed pot, combine the chopped strawberries, sugar, lime juice, and lime zest.
3. Stir the mixture well to combine.
4. Place the pot over medium-high heat and bring the mixture to a full rolling boil, stirring constantly.
5. Reduce the heat to medium-low and let the mixture simmer, stirring occasionally, until it thickens and reaches the desired consistency. This typically takes about 20-30 minutes.
6. To test if the jam is ready, place a small amount on a chilled plate and let it cool for a minute. If it wrinkles when you push it with your finger, it's ready.
7. Once the jam reaches the desired consistency, remove the pot from the heat.
8. Stir in the coconut milk and vanilla extract until well combined.
9. Ladle the hot jam into prepared jars, leaving about 1/4 inch of headspace.
10. Wipe the rims of the jars with a clean, damp cloth to remove any residue.
11. Place the lids on the jars and screw on the bands until fingertip tight.
12. Process the filled jars in a boiling water canner for 10 minutes (adjust for altitude if necessary).
13. Remove the jars from the canner and let them cool completely at room temperature. Check the seals before storing.
14. Store the jars in a cool, dark place for up to a year. Once opened, store in the refrigerator and use within a few weeks.

This Strawberry Coconut Jam is perfect for spreading on toast, muffins, or scones, or for using as a topping for yogurt or oatmeal. Enjoy the tropical flavors!

**Mango Lime Chili Jam**

Ingredients:

- 4 cups (about 600g) ripe mangoes, peeled, pitted, and chopped
- 1 cup (200g) granulated sugar
- Juice and zest of 2 limes
- 1-2 red chili peppers, finely chopped (adjust to taste)
- Pinch of salt

Instructions:

1. Prepare your canning jars and lids according to proper canning procedures.
2. In a large, heavy-bottomed pot, combine the chopped mangoes, sugar, lime juice, lime zest, chopped chili peppers, and a pinch of salt.
3. Stir the mixture well to combine.
4. Place the pot over medium-high heat and bring the mixture to a full rolling boil, stirring constantly.
5. Reduce the heat to medium-low and let the mixture simmer, stirring occasionally, until it thickens and reaches the desired consistency. This typically takes about 20-30 minutes.
6. To test if the jam is ready, place a small amount on a chilled plate and let it cool for a minute. If it wrinkles when you push it with your finger, it's ready.
7. Once the jam reaches the desired consistency, remove the pot from the heat.
8. Ladle the hot jam into prepared jars, leaving about 1/4 inch of headspace.
9. Wipe the rims of the jars with a clean, damp cloth to remove any residue.
10. Place the lids on the jars and screw on the bands until fingertip tight.
11. Process the filled jars in a boiling water canner for 10 minutes (adjust for altitude if necessary).
12. Remove the jars from the canner and let them cool completely at room temperature. Check the seals before storing.
13. Store the jars in a cool, dark place for up to a year. Once opened, store in the refrigerator and use within a few weeks.

This Mango Lime Chili Jam is perfect for spreading on toast, sandwiches, or crackers, or for using as a glaze for grilled meats or seafood. Enjoy the sweet, tangy, and spicy flavors!

**Pineapple Sage Jam**

Ingredients:

- 4 cups (about 600g) diced fresh pineapple
- 1 cup (200g) granulated sugar
- Juice and zest of 1 lemon
- 2 tablespoons chopped fresh sage leaves

Instructions:

1. Prepare your canning jars and lids according to proper canning procedures.
2. In a large, heavy-bottomed pot, combine the diced pineapple, sugar, lemon juice, lemon zest, and chopped sage leaves.
3. Stir the mixture well to combine.
4. Place the pot over medium-high heat and bring the mixture to a full rolling boil, stirring constantly.
5. Reduce the heat to medium-low and let the mixture simmer, stirring occasionally, until it thickens and reaches the desired consistency. This typically takes about 20-30 minutes.
6. To test if the jam is ready, place a small amount on a chilled plate and let it cool for a minute. If it wrinkles when you push it with your finger, it's ready.
7. Once the jam reaches the desired consistency, remove the pot from the heat.
8. Ladle the hot jam into prepared jars, leaving about 1/4 inch of headspace.
9. Wipe the rims of the jars with a clean, damp cloth to remove any residue.
10. Place the lids on the jars and screw on the bands until fingertip tight.
11. Process the filled jars in a boiling water canner for 10 minutes (adjust for altitude if necessary).
12. Remove the jars from the canner and let them cool completely at room temperature. Check the seals before storing.
13. Store the jars in a cool, dark place for up to a year. Once opened, store in the refrigerator and use within a few weeks.

This Pineapple Sage Jam is perfect for spreading on toast, muffins, or scones, or for using as a glaze for meats or roasted vegetables. Enjoy the tropical and herbal flavors!

**Orange Ginger Jam**

Ingredients:

- 4 cups (about 600g) oranges (about 4 medium-sized oranges)
- 1 tablespoon grated fresh ginger
- 2 cups (400g) granulated sugar
- Juice of 1 lemon
- Zest of 1 orange (optional)

Instructions:

1. Prepare your canning jars and lids according to proper canning procedures.
2. Wash the oranges thoroughly. Cut them in half and squeeze out the juice. Remove any seeds and set aside.
3. Chop the orange peels into small pieces. If desired, you can remove the white pith from the peels, but it's not necessary.
4. In a large, heavy-bottomed pot, combine the chopped orange peels, grated ginger, sugar, lemon juice, and orange zest (if using).
5. Stir the mixture well to combine.
6. Place the pot over medium-high heat and bring the mixture to a full rolling boil, stirring constantly.
7. Reduce the heat to medium-low and let the mixture simmer, stirring occasionally, until it thickens and reaches the desired consistency. This typically takes about 30-40 minutes.
8. To test if the jam is ready, place a small amount on a chilled plate and let it cool for a minute. If it wrinkles when you push it with your finger, it's ready.
9. Once the jam reaches the desired consistency, remove the pot from the heat.
10. Ladle the hot jam into prepared jars, leaving about 1/4 inch of headspace.
11. Wipe the rims of the jars with a clean, damp cloth to remove any residue.
12. Place the lids on the jars and screw on the bands until fingertip tight.
13. Process the filled jars in a boiling water canner for 10 minutes (adjust for altitude if necessary).
14. Remove the jars from the canner and let them cool completely at room temperature. Check the seals before storing.
15. Store the jars in a cool, dark place for up to a year. Once opened, store in the refrigerator and use within a few weeks.

This Orange Ginger Jam is perfect for spreading on toast, scones, or muffins, or for using as a glaze for meats or roasted vegetables. Enjoy the bright and zesty flavors with a hint of warmth from the ginger!

www.ingramcontent.com/pod-product-compliance
Lightning Source LLC
LaVergne TN
LVHW081318060526
838201LV00055B/2333